Minute Help Guides Presents:

A Newbies Guide to iPod Nano

SOME PEOPLE ONLY HAVE A FEW MINUTES TO SPARE

Minute Help Guides

Minute Help Press

www.minutehelp.com

Cover Image © Tan Kian Khoon - Fotolia.com.

Table of Contents

Introduction

The iPod Nano has been through seven different iterations since its introduction in 2006. Perhaps even more so than with the much-heralded iPhone and iPad, the Nano is Apple's favorite device to experiment with: larger capacities, different screens, complete redesign – the Nano has been a lot of different things over the years. But this seventh generation is something else entirely – a multi-touch powerhouse that features pretty much everything you'd ever want in an MP3 player, and a few things you didn't even *know* you'd need.

This guide will take you through the ins and outs of the iPod Nano – from working with iTunes to using the built-in pedometer. We'll show you everything you need to know, saving the fluff for people who have time to waste.

Ready? Let's do this!

Part One: Introducing the New iPod Nano

The iPod Revolution: a Short History

In the prehistoric days before ubiquitous computers and DVD Burners (the 1970s), The LP record was king. For the uninitiated among you, LP records were 12 inch round discs with little grooves in them. They were pretty much the only way people consumed music at home for much of the 20th century. LPs looked like this:

The great thing about LPs, at least for the music industry, was the expense. Difficult to manufacture and even more difficult to steal, consumers had basically no choice but to buy millions of copies of the best records. Sure, you could loan one to a friend, but they'd have to return it eventually, right? Blank records that could be recorded onto weren't a thing the average consumer could afford, so the music was protected, so to speak.

In the late 70s, Phillips brought to market an item that would forever change the musical landscape. The cassette, as it came to be known, relied on magnetic tape inside a casing, rather than the grooves of an LP. A much smaller medium, cassettes became hugely popular with the introduction of portable cassette players, most notably the Walkman. The music industry embraced cassette tapes, and the market was split pretty much evenly between LPs and cassettes for a while.

But all was not well in cassette land. As an open standard, development of the cassette was allowed by anyone who was interested, and Japanese cassette recorders, along with blank tapes, soon flooded the market. Recordable cassettes meant that people could copy their LPs (and other cassettes) to a blank tape, removing the need for consumers to purchase a copy of their own.

This, of course, became a hugely popular thing to do. Cassettes were cheap, less than a dollar each in most cases, and could be recorded on over and over again. People recorded their favorite songs off the radio, off their friends' records, and even from the air around them at concerts. Needless to say, the record companies were not happy. They sued virtually everyone they could. Of course, Pandora already opened the box – there was no going back. The record companies tried to appeal to the average music fan's sense of morality with a huge ad campaign:

This, as you can imagine, didn't do anything to stem the tide. After a while, things calmed down, and the record industry was fine. Music sales were the highest they'd ever been.

As the 1980s gave way to the 1990s, an even newer format came into popular use: the compact disc. Cheap to manufacture, but offering (for the first time) crystal clear digital sound, the record industry converted virtually their entire business to the CD within a few years. While people still could (and did) copy the music contained on CDs to blank cassettes, there was no way for the average consumer to make their own CDs, so people who copied the music would be getting a pale imitation of the CDs crystal clear sound. All was well.

If you haven't guessed by now, the computer revolution of the mid to late 1990s added CD (and then DVD) drives to millions of American households. Blank CDs were even cheaper than cassettes, costing only pennies each. People began to copy each other's CDs in record numbers, creating perfect digital replicas of store-bought CDs.

This time, the record industry didn't bother to freak out. They'd weathered this kind of storm twice before, and hadn't suffered any lasting ill-effects. This time was different.

As computers became more powerful, people began to take the CDs they purchased from the store and make digital copies on their computers, eschewing the blank CD entirely. In the late 1990s, the MP3 became the file format of choice for this "ripped" music. The concurrent rise of the Internet made music piracy a global phenomenon. People began to trade and collect MP3s as fast as their connections would allow. Then, in 1999, a bomb went off. The bomb was named Napster.

Developed by a well-meaning college kid named Shawn Fanning, Napster was a peer-to-peer networking application that allowed people to share their entire MP3 collections with the entire world. At its peak, over 100 million people were using the service to download and upload MP3s of everything from pre-release copies of major albums to old and out-of-print music unavailable anywhere else.

The record industry sued, musicians sued, pretty much everybody sued. This time they won, shutting down Napster in 2001. But it was a pyrrhic victory – dozens of other services followed in Napster's footsteps, making sure that the MP3 was here to stay. People, it turned out, were not about to give up on the convenience of digital music.

Right around this time, Apple CEO Steve Jobs had a grand vision for his company, centered on this new world of digital content. The MP3 was still steadily gaining in popularity, even inspiring some (terrible) portable players. These devices, notably the Creative Nomad and the Archos Jukebox, were clunky devices with limited battery life and absolutely appalling user interfaces.

Despite the objections and protestations of the record companies, Apple worked steadily (and secretly) on a device of their own for a couple of years. In late 2001, they unleashed the first iPod upon the world, immediately capturing the hearts and minds of millions of Apple devotees. Billed as "1,000 songs in your pocket", the original iPod was everything that its (long-forgotten) competitors were not: sleek, simple to use, and easy to manage.

The management part was taken care of by iTunes, an Apple program designed to help organize consumers' growing MP3 collections. Users (initially limited only to Apple-produced Macintosh computers) could even convert their existing CDs to the MP3 format at the touch of a button, copy them to their iPod, and voila! 1,000 songs were in your pocket. A copy of iTunes came pre-installed on every computer Apple sold from that point on, helping to make sure that everyone, even people who weren't already onboard with MP3s, had the power at their fingertips.

An innovative ad campaign followed, cementing the iPod as the "it" device of the decade before Windows users could even buy it for themselves.

Capitalizing on the success of the iPod, Apple continued to release new iterations of it – the iPod mini, the iPod Nano, the iPod Shuffle. To go along with all of these new devices, they began refining iTunes like crazy, moving from version 1.0 to 7.0 in just a few years.

Along the way, they convinced the (now desperate) record companies that they could help them sell music, rather than just be a receptacle for pirated MP3s. After securing permission, they added the iTunes Music Store, where people could purchase MP3 files for $.99 each, or entire albums for $9.99. By integrating the purchase into the software, Apple taught a whole generation of people that purchasing music was still the right thing to do.

*The iPod also created an entirely new art form: the podcast. A portmanteau of 'iPod' and 'Broadcast', podcasts are sort of like radio shows, released to iTunes whenever a podcaster likes, on a subscription basis. We'll discuss the awesome-sauce that is the podcasting world a little later in this guide.

From this point, the story becomes a little more familiar. Apple would go on to practically own the digital media world, selling consumers everything from music to television shows, with books, movies, and apps thrown in for good measure. The iPhone and the iPad took the iPod concept and ran with it – first for the telephone, then for the touch screen tablet. But everything still comes back to the iPod, the idea that started it all. That's where the iPod Nano fits in – it's the only device left that stays true to the original while adding in all the bells and whistles that Apple enthusiasts have come to expect.

What's in the Box (and what isn't)

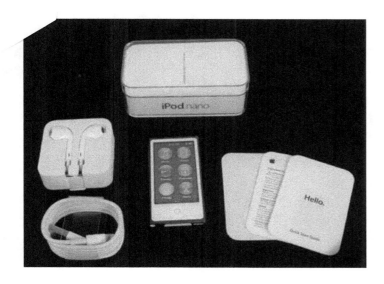

As with all Apple products, your new iPod Nano comes in a pretty elegant package – every piece seamlessly placed inside a small, minimalist cube of plastic that's not much larger than the device itself. Inside, you'll find several different items:

- The iPod Nano itself (in a rainbow of possible colors)
- A set of Apple's new "EarPods" (though a somewhat 'lesser' version of these than is included with the iPhone 5)
- A "Lightning" to USB adapter
- A "Quick Start" Guide and an Apple sticker

Now, this is pretty much everything you'll need to get started, with two small exceptions. You might want to pick up these (relatively) low-cost items to complete the experience.

The first item you might want to pick up to get the most out of your iPod Nano is a set of EarPods with player controls on them. Apple sells a version of these, and also includes them with their new iPhone and iPod Touch devices. These headphones look almost identical to the ear Pods included with your iPod Nano, but they have a small piece of plastic that looks like this:

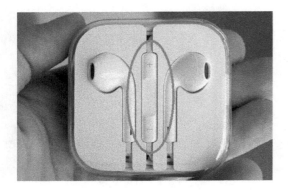

This can be used to raise and lower the volume, change songs, play and pause the device, and pretty much anything else you can do without having to look at your iPod Nano's screen. This can come in handy when using the device on the go, while jogging, or even at the gym. Check out Apple.com or Amazon for pricing, but a set these more advanced Ear Pods cost around $29 bucks at the time of this writing. These headphones also include a small built-in microphone, which will come in handy if you ever need to use them as a hands-free device for your smartphone.

The second thing that's not included in the iPod Nano packaging is a USB wall charger. While the USB port on any computer is suitable for charging the device, plugging it into an outlet will charge the device in about half the time, which can be awfully convenient. Of course, we can't fault Apple for this omission, as wall chargers tend to be big, and most consumers already have one or two of them in their home. The wall charger for any other device (like Amazon's Kindle, for example) will work just fine with the iPod Nano. If you don't happen to have one, there are (again) options for a dollar or two on sites like Amazon.com or even in most electronics stores.

The last, and perhaps least obvious, thing that's missing within the iPod Nano packaging is the software needed to use it. We'll get to the downloading and installation of iTunes a little later in this guide. For now, let's dig a little deeper and discuss the iPod Nano hardware.

The iPod Nano Hardware

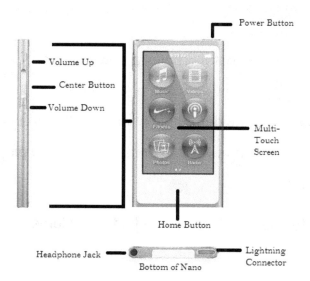

As you can see from the above illustration, there are several components to the iPod Nano hardware. While we'll go over the specific functions of the device a little later in this guide, let's take a second to learn a little bit about it before diving in.

The hardware of your iPod Nano is broken up into several different areas of the device. Along the top, you'll find the power button. This is used to turn the device on and off, and also to turn on the screen. Below that, you'll find a 2.5 inch multi-touch screen. We'll discuss this at length a little later in this guide. Below that, you'll find what Apple refers to as the Home button. This is a familiar item to anyone who's ever used an iPhone, iPad, or iPod touch.

On the bottom of the device, you'll find two important things. First, you'll find the headphone port on the left hand side. This is where you'll plug your headphones in and is the only way to listen to audio, as there is no external speaker.

On the right side of the bottom, you'll find the 'Lightning' connector. This is a new thing for Apple, available (thus far) only on this device and the brand new versions of the iPhone and iPad. It's a pretty neat connector, but not compatible with the older 30 pin connector that many iPod accessories were designed for. The best part of this connector is that it, unlike the 30 pin, has no 'right' side, meaning you can plug it in in either direction.

The last section we need to cover is the left side of the device. Here, you'll find the volume rocker and the center button. Use the volume up button to turn the device's volume up, and use the volume down button to turn it down. The center button acts as a play/pause button, allowing you to start and stop the playing of your content without having to use the touchscreen.

That's all there is to the iPod Nano hardware. In the next section we'll dig a little deeper and take you through the process of installing and setting up iTunes – the software that your iPod Nano relies on to interact with your computer.

Part Two: Working With iTunes

Downloading/Installing iTunes

Before we get started using the iPod Nano, we'll have to set up the program that allows us to use the device with our computer. Users of Apple computers have the luxury of a pre-installed version of iTunes on their systems. For the rest of us, we've got to install it ourselves. While the rest of this guide is basically applicable to both operating systems, this particular section is just for the Windows folks.

While many (maybe even most) companies will include the software in the box the hardware came in, Apple does not share this philosophy. A lot of the relative sparseness inside your average package from Apple is meant as a nod to their "green" initiatives. After all, if you've bought a device that you're going to connect to your computer anyway, why include a CD that you might not use? To that end, in order to get started with iTunes, we're going to have to head to the Internet.

Even though iTunes is required to interact with our iPod Nano, there's a whole lot more to the program than that. ITunes also includes a built-in music store and access to both Podcasts and educational content from iTunes U, which we'll discuss a little later in this guide.

First things first: there are some basic minimum requirements your computer needs to meet in order to even *run* the iTunes software. While most modern computers will almost definitely pass muster, you should probably make sure before going ahead. Here's what your computer needs to *run* iTunes:

- 1Ghz or faster processor
- At least 512MB of ram
- A DirectX 9.0 compatible video card

- A monitor with a resolution of at least 1024x768

Now, there are a few additional things that, while not exactly requirements, are pretty much essential for getting any use out of iTunes. In order to play HD video or use iTunes LP or iTunes Extras, you'll need to have the following:

- 2Ghz Core 2 Duo (or faster) processor
- At least 1GB of ram (2GB for 1080p video)
- Intel GMA 3000 (or better) video card
- A 16 bit sound card w/ speaker
- A broadband Internet Connection

Now, you'll also have to be using a relatively modern version of Windows to install iTunes. You'll have to upgrade if you're not using *at least* Windows XP with Service Pack 2. Seeing as how that operating system is over 10 years old at this point, we'll go ahead and assume that this doesn't apply to very many people at this point.

Now that we've made sure our computer equipment is up to snuff, let's get down to business. To get started with installing iTunes 11, point your web browser to www.itunes.com. Once you've done that, you'll be greeted with this screen:

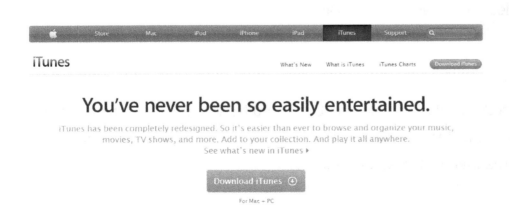

From here, all you need to do is click the blue box labeled 'Download iTunes'. Once you've done that, you'll be taken to a second screen with some more details. That will look like this:

Download iTunes

iTunes 11.0.2 for Windows (64-bit)

☑ Email me New On iTunes and special iTunes offers.

☑ Keep me up to date with Apple news, software updates, and the latest information on products and services.

Apple Customer Privacy Policy

Email Address

Download Now ⊙

As you can see, the website automatically detected which version of Windows we were using. This works 90% of the time, but it's a good idea to double check that you're downloading the 64 bit version if you're using a 64 bit version of Windows. To do this, just right click on the 'computer' icon in any explorer window to bring up the system information. You'll find either 32-bit or 64-bit operating system under the heading 'system type'.

As you can see, Apple would like to add your email address to a couple different mailing lists. Normally we'd tell you to go ahead and uncheck those boxes – but Apple does frequently run some pretty stunning sales on iTunes, and you'll likely miss them if you don't get the emails. We'll leave it up to you.

Once you've done that, click the blue box labeled 'Download Now' to begin downloading the iTunes software. It's a little under 90 megabytes in size, which should only take a couple of minutes on a standard broadband internet connection.

Depending on your web browser, you may have to give permission to download the application. Once you've done that, you'll find it wherever your web browser puts downloaded files, which is usually (but not always!) in the 'downloads' folder. If you're having trouble finding the file, just open the start menu and search for it. The file will be named either iTunes32setup.exe or iTunes64setup.exe and it'll look like this within the explorer window:

iTunes64Setup
iTunes Installer
Apple Inc.

Once you've found the file, double-click it to open it and begin the installation process. Depending on your security settings, you'll probably have to give Windows permission to open the program. This permission request will come in the form of a pop-up window that looks like this:

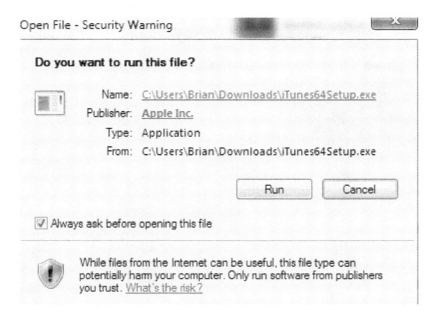

We can obviously trust Apple not to send us viruses, so go ahead and click 'run' to continue. Once you've done that, the setup program will begin its preparations. Hang back for a minute while it runs through this screen:

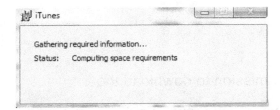

Once it's finished, you'll be greeted with the 'Welcome to iTunes' installer screen. This screen only exists as a chance to stop the installation. Tap 'Next' to proceed.

Once you've done that, you'll be presented with the 'installation options' screen. Here, you have a couple of options. You can choose to add a shortcut to iTunes on your desktop (go ahead, unless you're a desktop neat freak), make iTunes the default player for all of your audio files (this doesn't actually seem to work, so we'll have to it ourselves in the next section anyway).

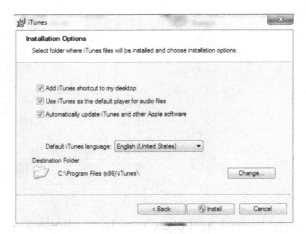

You'll also be given a choice between automatically updating iTunes or doing it yourself (manually). On this point, we recommend unchecking that box. From time to time, an update will have bugs that haven't been worked out yet – we think it's better to update iTunes ourselves, after making sure that everything is copacetic.

Once you've made your decisions, click 'install' to initiate the installation process. Be patient – it'll take a few minutes. During the wait, Apple will display a couple of images touting various iTunes features. Just hang back and let it do its thing.

After a few minutes, you'll be greeted with the 'installation complete' screen:

From here, you can choose whether or not to open iTunes immediately after exiting the installer. Go ahead and leave that box checked, as we'll be diving right in to the software. Click 'finish' to complete the installation and launch iTunes.

That's all there is to it.

Setting Everything Up/The iTunes 11 Interface

Now that we've installed the iTunes 11 software and clicked 'finished', iTunes will automatically open for the first time. Before we can really dive in to the program, we have to go through a few more hurdles. First up: the iTunes Software License Agreement. This should pop up automatically a second or two after we click 'finish'.

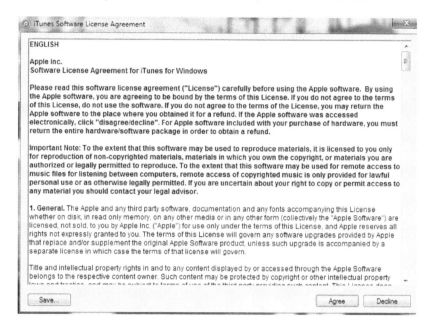

As you can see, there's a whole lot of reading to do. We'd *like* to say that every word of this is crucial for you to understand, but the truth is that it's just boilerplate legal mumbo-jumbo. You can just tap 'agree' and move on.

> *How do we know this? We actually wasted a half-hour of our lives reading through the entire thing. We might actually be the first to have ever done so. Trust us, it's not a thrilling read, and you're not missing anything.*

Once you've clicked 'agree', you'll (more than likely) be greeted with the following pop-up:

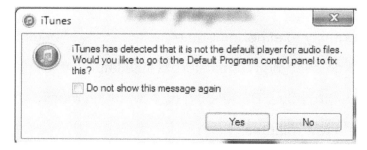

As you can see, iTunes is *not* actually the default player for audio files, despite the fact that we checked the appropriate box when installing the software. It's confusing – and maybe a little annoying – but don't worry; it's an easy fix. Just tap 'Yes' to set this feature up.

Once you've done that, you'll be greeted with the default programs menu. Find the menu item labeled 'select all' in the middle of the screen. Once you've done that, click 'save'. *Now* we've set iTunes as the default player for audio files.

Once you've finished with that, you'll be greeted with yet another pop-up from iTunes. This time, you're simply giving permission for Apple to look through whatever MP3s you have in order to sort them and automatically retrieve album covers and other info, saving you a little legwork. Just click 'agree' to let this happen.

Once you've done that, you'll be given the opportunity to either enter the iTunes store or begin scanning for the music on your hard drive. We'll go over the iTunes store a little later in this guide, so for right now, just let iTunes scan your hard drive. Depending on how much music you're storing on your computer, this might take a few minutes.

Music

Songs and music videos you add to iTunes appear in your Music library. Your music purchases in iCloud will also appear whenever you're signed into the iTunes Store.

Go to the iTunes Store   Scan for Media

Once that's finished, you're all set up. All that's left to do is navigate our way around the iTunes 11 interface. To get started, let's first take a look at the top of the program screen. This is where we'll be doing most of our navigating from.

As you can see, there are several parts to this interface. First, let's discuss that little box in the corner. This is where the traditional *file, edit, etc.* menu system usually seen in Windows programs resides. Click it once to take a look at what's inside.

- New – this area is where playlists are created. We'll go over playlists in a later section of this guide.
- Library – this area is reserved for home sharing and manually downloading album artwork.

- ITunes Store—this is where we'll interact with our iTunes account, including the authorization of our various computers and devices.

- Add File to Library – for files you'd like to manually add to the iTunes library after the initial search that we just performed, this is where we'll do that.

- Get Info – this menu item is context dependent. If you've selected an item within iTunes, you'll be able to get its information, and edit it if you choose. More on that a little later.

- Switch to MiniPlayer – iTunes comes with a smaller, unobtrusive player, for use when you're doing other things with your computer. Clicking here will activate it.

- Preferences – this section contains all of the advanced features and settings for iTunes 11. We'll get in-depth with this in a moment.

- Show Menu Bar – click here to activate the traditional Windows-style *file, edit, view* type menu system. It's a good idea to enable that now, as we'll be going over it shortly.

- Exit – clicking here will exit the iTunes 11 program.

Now, below the little box in the corner, you'll see an icon that's labeled 'Music'. Click it, and you'll see that it expands to include four selectable categories: Music, Movies, TV Shows, and Home Sharing.

These items are, in essence, your library of content. Since we've only just started the program, the only library that will have any content in it will be your Music library, which is now full of whatever music was on your hard drive that iTunes automatically detected. Below the Library Menu, you'll find all of your content, which will look something like this:

On the right hand side of the screen, you'll find a button labeled 'iTunes Store'. Clicking here will switch the program's functionality from media player to media store, and clicking it again will switch it back. But let's not get ahead of ourselves. Before we explore the iTunes Store, we'll have to set it up.

Ready? Let's go!

Part Three: Using iTunes

The iTunes Store

Now that we've learned a little bit about the iTunes 11 interface, let's go ahead and set up the iTunes Store so we can begin browsing for new content to add. This section primarily applies to folks who've never had an iTunes account – those who have can simply sign in and skip the following tutorial.

To get started with the iTunes Store, go ahead and click the 'iTunes Store' button on the upper right hand side of the program. Once you do, the interface will now look something like this:

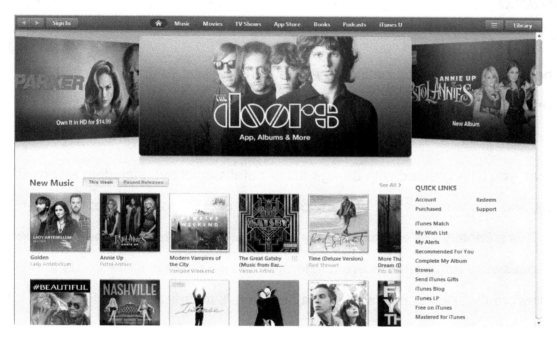

In the upper left-hand corner of the screen, you'll now find a button labeled 'Sign In'. Tap it to begin the account creation process. You'll be greeted with a pop-up screen that looks like this:

If you've already got an Apple ID, great. Just sign in and you're done. For those who don't, however, click the button on the bottom left that's labeled 'Create Apple ID'. Once you've done that, you'll be taken back to the main window of the iTunes 11 program, which will now look like this:

With an Apple ID, you can download the latest music, videos, and more.

To begin creating your Apple ID, click Continue.

In previous versions of iTunes, all of these various screens that appear within the main window were actually separate things. This new emphasis on 'unification' makes things a lot simpler than in previous iterations. Lucky us!

Click 'Continue' to begin the process of creating an Apple ID. Once you've done that, you'll be presented with yet another 'Terms and Conditions' page that you'll have to agree to. Check the box labeled 'I have read and agree to the terms and conditions' and click 'Continue' again.

Once you've done that, you'll be greeted with a page full of details to fill out, including an email address, a password, and answers to a few 'security questions' in case you ever get locked out of your account. This is mostly like anything else you've ever signed up for online, with one major exception: the password requirements are a little bit, shall we say, strict. It took us a few tries to land on a password that Apple approved of. In fact, here's their list of rules for the initial password you create:

Password must:
- ○ Have at least one letter
- ○ Have at least one capital letter
- ○ Have at least one number
- ◉ Not contain multiple identical consecutive characters
- ◉ Not be the same as the account name
- ○ Be at least 8 characters

In short, Apple *really* cares about the security of your account. Once you've created your bulletproof password and entered in the rest of the information, click 'Continue' to be taken to the payment method page. Enter your credit card (or PayPal) information and your billing address, and click 'Create Apple ID' to finish the process.

Once that's done, you'll be automatically logged into your iTunes account. You'll see your account ID in the left hand corner of the screen:

Click here at any time to look at (or edit) your account details, sign out, or redeem iTunes gift cards.

Now that we've set up our iTunes account, let's take a look at how everything works. Remember, any time you'd like to return to your library, just click that same button in the right hand corner of the screen, which is now labeled – appropriately enough – 'Library'.

As we touched on briefly a little earlier in this guide, you can now see the seven mini-stores that make up the iTunes Store. They're right there along the top of the screen, next to the icon that looks like a house. Clicking this 'Home' icon will take you to a sort of overview of all the stores. This is mostly just advertising for the 'featured' items in each store, but it gives a good overview of the sheer breadth of content available.

In addition to these items, you'll find some helpful stuff along the right hand side. Here, you'll see various iTunes Charts – the most purchased/downloaded items in the store.

Clicking on any of the specific mini-store labels at the top will limit the store to *just* that content, giving you a more detailed overview of what's available. Clicking on any item within the store will bring up that item's details. For example, we clicked on "Push the Sky Away", the new album from the critically acclaimed group Nick Cave and the Bad Seeds. We were greeted with this page:

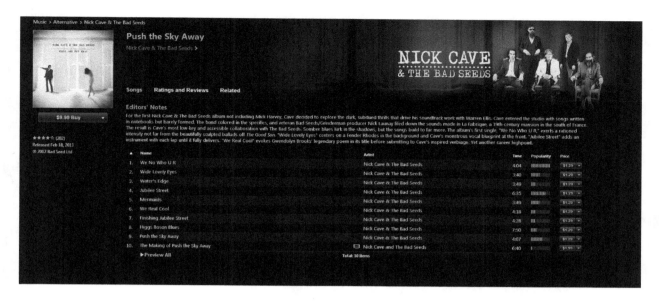

As you can see, there's a *ton* of information here. This is the case for pretty much every album in the entire catalog. You'll see a brief description under the heading 'Editors Notes' as well as the track listing in the middle of the screen. Each individual song can be previewed by clicking the track number. Once clicked, the track will immediately begin to play in iTunes without leaving the page. For most songs, you'll be given a 90 second preview.

To the right of each track, you'll see a link to purchase the individual songs. While this is true for most albums in the iTunes catalog, some songs from some artists are labeled 'album only' and cannot be previewed or purchased individually.

Single songs can be purchased for $1.29, while full albums are generally a little bit cheaper than the sum of the tracks. Interestingly, iTunes will give you the option to 'complete your album' by purchasing the rest of the tracks for the difference in price between what you've already purchased and the price of the album. In the example above, we could purchase a single song at $1.29, and then later purchase the rest of the album for only $8.70.

Once you've purchased an item, it will begin downloading immediately. As soon as it's finished, it will appear within your iTunes library, ready to use and copy over to your iPod Nano.

In the next section, we'll begin to use the iPod Nano, copy some music and video to it, and discuss some of its more advanced features.

Part Four: Using iPod Nano

Connecting iPod Nano for the First Time

Now that we've installed (and learned a bit about) iTunes, it's time to begin using the iPod Nano. To get started, plug the USB cable into an available USB port on your computer, and then plug the 3.5mm end into the headphone port of your device.

> *The next couple of paragraphs assume that you're using a Windows computer. If you're using a Mac, just open iTunes after you've plugged in the device and follow along from there.*

Once you've done that, you'll be greeted with the 'installing device driver' bubble in the bottom right corner of your desktop:

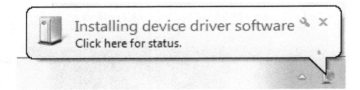

This is Windows figuring out what you've just plugged in. Once it's finished, you'll be greeted with this pop-up:

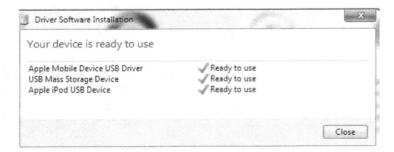

Click 'close' to finish the installation process. ITunes should automatically open at this point. If it doesn't, just launch the program from the start menu. Once you've done that, you'll be shown the new iPod setup screen, which will look like this:

Click 'continue' to begin.

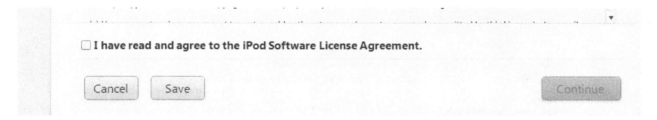

The first thing you'll have to do is agree to the terms and conditions (again). Click the check box and tap 'continue' to move on. Once you've done that, you'll be shown a quick walk-through page, covering the various ways you'll be interacting with the iPod Nano from within iTunes.

Click 'continue' to move on. You'll be greeted with another 'get started' page. Click 'Get Started' to move on.

Once you've done that, you'll be taken to the iPod Nano summary page. We'll be doing a couple of things from here, starting with applying an update to the Nano's software:

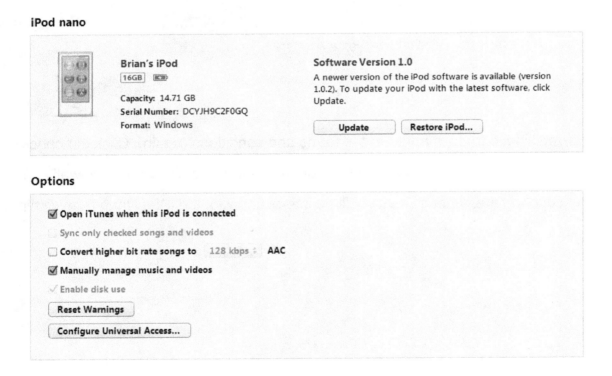

All you need to do here is click the 'Update' button. Once you've done that, you'll be presented with a pop-up window describing the update. Click 'Next' to begin the process.

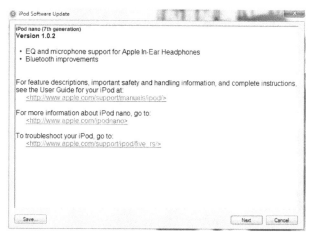 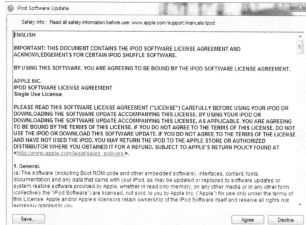

Once you've done that, you'll be taken to yet another 'terms' agreement type page. Click 'agree' to move on. The update will begin downloading immediately. You can check the progress of the download by checking out the info screen in the middle of the iTunes window:

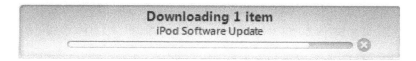

Once it's finished downloading, a pop-up window will come up, informing you that the device is updating:

When it's finished updating, you'll be greeted with *yet another* pop-up window informing you of that fact:

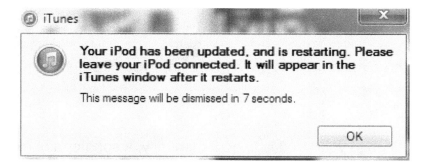

After your iPod Nano reboots, iTunes will ask you to register the device with your Apple ID. This can come in handy if you ever need customer support. Click 'register' to do this now, or

'Later' if you're not interested. If you've clicked 'register', all you need to do is provide the Apple ID and password we created earlier. The rest will be done for you.

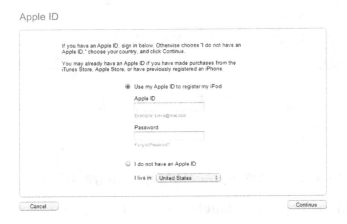

Adding Music to Your iPod Nano

Now that we've got our iPod Nano all set up, it's time to start adding some music to the device. There are a few different ways to do this, all of them pretty easy to do.

From the 'Summary' view that we entered upon finishing the setup, find the button labeled 'Done' and click it. This will take us back to the library view.

As you can see, your library view is a little bit different now. In addition to the buttons for 'iTunes Store' and the various libraries, you'll now have an 'iPod' icon that looks like this:

Click that icon at any time to return to the iPod summary view.

Now that that's sorted, let's discuss the three main ways to get content onto your iPod.

Manually

The most common method for copying things to your iPod is to do it manually, a song or album at a time. It's also the simplest way. To copy a song manually, just click to highlight the song, and then drag it over to the right side of the screen:

As you can see, a 'devices' pain will automatically open up on the right hand side of the screen. To copy a song to the iPod, just drag it to that device. You'll see a red number icon – this is to tell you how many songs you're currently copying over.

To copy an entire album to the iPod, just drag the album cover over to the right in the same way. As you can see, copying is the same as it is for a single song, with the exception of that red number. This time, the number is 13 – the number of songs on the album that we're copying over.

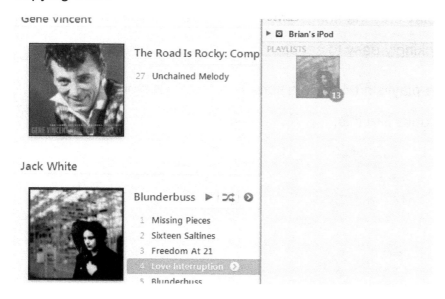

To copy a bunch of different songs all at once, just highlight one of the songs, and then press the CTRL button on your keyboard. Click to highlight any other songs you want to copy, all while continuing to hold the CTRL button. When you've highlighted everything you want to copy over, just drag one of the highlighted items to the right – all of the songs will copy over, giving you whatever amount you're copying as that magic red number:

Using Playlists

The playlist concept is one of the coolest features of iTunes. We've got a bunch of music in our library, ready to copy over to our iPod Nano. We can do copy over albums, songs, or even entire artists. But what about those times when you want to listen to a mixture of a bunch of different stuff? Enter playlists.

Playlists are, in the simplest of terms, files that iTunes uses to create customized albums. You can create a playlist and fill it with any song in your library, in any order you choose. Once you begin playing a playlist, iTunes will play only the songs you've added, and only in the order you want. Pretty cool, huh? It's also shockingly easy to set up.

To get started with playlists, click the playlists tab on the library menu. Once you've done that, you'll be greeted with a screen that looks like this:

As you can see, playlists are kept on the left hand side, while the items within the playlist take up the middle of the screen. By default, there are six different playlists listed in this section. These are really just suggestions from Apple. To begin creating your own playlist, head to the bottom left of the screen. There you'll find a button labeled with the + symbol.

Click the + sign, and then click 'New Playlist'. Once you've done that, you'll be taken to the playlist creation screen.

The first thing you'll want to do is give the playlist a name. You can choose anything you like here, but it's generally a good idea to use something that's descriptive like "Slow Jams" or "Best of Bananarama", which will help us when we activate VoiceOver a little bit later.

Once you've decided on a name for your playlist, just click on any song in the main part of the screen and drag it to the right. Once you've done that, the song is added to the playlist. That's all there is to it.

To add multiple songs at one time, simply click on one song, press the ctrl button and click on the other songs you'd like to add. Once you've chosen all the songs you'd like to add, drag one to the right and all of the songs will be added.

Instead of dragging, you can also right-click on a selection, which will bring up this context menu:

From there, find the menu item labeled 'Add to Playlist' and choose the playlist you'd like to add the songs to.

Once you've added some songs, rearrange them into any order you like by dragging the files on the right up or down in the list:

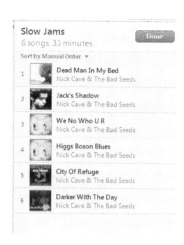

When you've finished creating your playlist, click 'done' to exit the playlist editor. Then, to copy the playlist to your iPod, just click into Playlist view, find your playlist and drag it to the right, just as you would a single song or album:

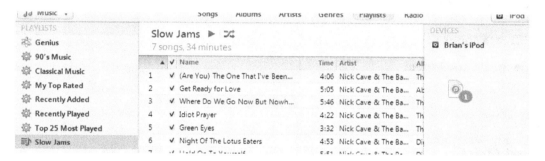

Drag it up to the iPod icon to copy the playlist to the device.

Syncing

If copying files and playlists over to your iPod seems like too much of a hassle, Apple does have an easier way. ITunes will allow you to sync *everything* in your library to any device, updating it as you add or delete files (and plug in the device). Since the iPod Nano only has 16GB worth of storage space, this is probably not a good option for people with large libraries of music. If you have less than a couple of gigs worth of audio, though, it can be incredibly convenient. Here's how to set it up:

Click the iPod icon to move to iPod Summary view:

Once you've done that, head to the 'options' section of the page, and find the item labeled

'Manually Manage Music and Videos'.

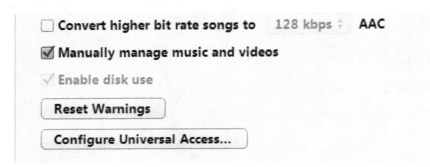

Uncheck the checkbox to change the iPod to syncing mode. Once you've done that, a pop-up window will show up, asking you to confirm.

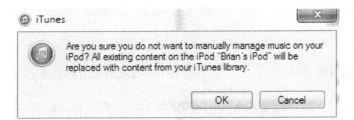

Now, it's important to note that anything you've copied to the iPod will be deleted when you click 'ok'. If you're comfortable with that, go ahead and click.

Once you've done that, all of your music will begin to copy over to the device. You can choose to exclude certain things by clicking over to the 'music' or 'podcast' tabs within the iPod Summary view:

Sync Music 0 songs

- ○ Entire music library
- ◉ Selected playlists, artists, albums, and genres
- ☐ Automatically fill free space with songs

Playlists

- ☐ ⚙ 90's Music
- ☐ ⚙ Classical Music
- ☐ ⚙ My Top Rated
- ☐ ⚙ Recently Added
- ☐ ⚙ Recently Played
- ☐ ⚙ Top 25 Most Played
- ☐ ♫ Slow Jams

Artists

- ☐ Dan Reeder
- ☐ Demented Are Go
- ☐ Flat Duo Jets
- ☐ Gene Vincent
- ☐ Jack White
- ☐ Nick Cave & The Bad Seeds
- ☐ Vampire Weekend
- ☐ Wanda Jackson
- ☐ The White Stripes

Genres

- ☐ Alternative
- ☐ Alternative Rock
- ☐ Indie Pop
- ☐ Post Punk
- ☐ Psychobilly
- ☐ Rock
- ☐ Rock/Pop
- ☐ Rockabilly

Albums

- ☐ Dan Reeder - Dan Reeder
- ☐ Demented Are Go - Hellbilly Storm
- ☐ Demented Are Go - Hellucifernation
- ☐ Demented Are Go - I Wanna See You Bleed!!
- ☐ Demented Are Go - In Sickness & In Health
- ☐ Demented Are Go - Kicked Out of Hell
- ☐ Demented Are Go - Orgasmic Nightmare
- ☐ Demented Are Go - Tangenital Madness on a Pleasant Side of...

Click the checkbox next to 'Entire Music Library' to sync everything, or check each box individually to check only what you want, sorted by genre, artist, album, or playlist.

Working with Video

In addition to its top-notch music playing function, your iPod Nano also functions as a video player. While the screen isn't exactly the largest thing available, it works better than you'd think.

The one caveat: the devices meant to work with iTunes (like the iPod Classic) will only play video files in one specific format called MPEG-4 (MP4 or M4V). While the videos sold in the iTunes store are always in this format, most videos downloaded or purchased elsewhere are not. Apple hasn't yet allowed iTunes to convert these files automatically, as they have with audio files, leaving those of you with other formats (like AVI or MKV) with no easy way of transferring this content to iTunes, and then to your iPod.

We can get around this in two ways. First, we can simply purchase all of our content through iTunes. This can get expensive pretty quickly. The second, and slightly more complicated method, is to take our existing DVDs (or AVI files) and convert them using third-party software.

There are a few options out there that will help you, but the gold standard is a free, open source piece of software called 'Handbrake'. While a full tutorial of the program is beyond the scope of this guide, there is a handy guide to all of this located at www.handbrake.fr. The rest of this section will assume that you've either purchased some iTunes video content or converted some of your own.

To copy video files to your iPod Nano, head to the 'Movies' or 'TV Shows' library in iTunes. Once there, find the video file(s) you'd like to copy over. Click once to highlight the file, and then drag the file to the right hand side of the screen. Just like with audio files, a separate section will show up, including an icon for your iPod. Drag the file up to the iPod icon, and note the red number.

Once you've copied the video file to your iPod, it will be viewable from the 'Videos' menu, separated by Movies, TV Shows, Rentals, and Music Videos (these menu items will only appear if you've copied these file types to the device). Tap on a video file to begin playing. The controls for the video work in exactly the same way as they do for audio.

But let's not get ahead of ourselves. Let's take a quick look at how you'll find your way around the iPod Nano, shall we?

The iPod Nano Interface

Now that we've copied some music and video files to the iPod Nano, let's discuss the software on the device, and how you'll interact with it. The iPod Nano is unique among Apple's devices – it doesn't use the old-school classic iPod interface, but it also doesn't use the more advanced iOS found on iPhones and iPads. Instead, you'll be using a sort-of hybrid of the two, which

Apple has cleverly dubbed Nano OS. There's not really a lot to it, but let's go over what you need to know.

To get started with the iPod Nano, press either the Home button (below the screen) or the power button (on top of the device) to turn the screen on. From there, you'll be greeted with the iPod Nano's home screen, which will look like this:

As we've already discussed, the iPod Nano's screen is touch-enabled. A lot of people have become perfectly familiar and comfortable with the way touch-screen devices work, but here's a quick primer for the uninitiated.

- Tapping and Double-Tapping – using your finger, you can tap on nearly any item on the screen. Tapping one of the app icons will open that app. Tapping a song (or video) within its category will begin playing the item. You can also double-tap certain items. By tapping twice in quick succession, you can zoom in on photos or change the size of a video while it's playing. You can also tap and hold any of the eight home screen icons to change the order in which they appear on the screen. To do this, just tap and hold until all the items begin to shake, then move the icon with your finger to where you'd like it to be. When you're finished moving things, tap the Home button to exit the rearrangement feature.

- Swiping – to move between home (and other) screens, place your finger at one end of the screen, then move it toward the other end of the screen in a continuous motion. Swipe from left to right within a menu to move back to the previous menu.

- Flicking – flicking is a lot like swiping, only in a vertical direction. Flick up or down to quickly scroll through a list of items (such as songs). The speed and intensity with which you flick will determine how fast and how far the scrolling will be. To stop the screen from scrolling, touch anywhere on the screen while it's still in motion.
- Pinching/Zooming – this is used exclusively in the photos section. Take your thumb and forefinger together and place them in the center of the screen, move them apart to zoom in on a picture, move them back together again to zoom out.

Now that we know how to interact with Nano OS, let's take a look at the various "apps" that make up the software. We're using the term "app" here for simplicity – these icons represent the various built-in functions of your device.

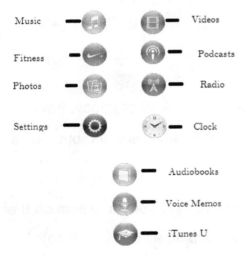

The above chart represents every possible item within your iPod Nano. The eight apps along the top are on the device by default, while the three at the bottom only show up when there is content of that type to display:

- Music – this is where all of your audio content will reside. The list of audio files is sortable by playlist, artist, album, song title, and genre. Any iTunes U or Podcast content will be located here, as well as the designated area for them.
- Fitness – this area holds the built-in fitness features, which we'll discuss a little later in this guide.
- Photos – this area will contain any pictures you sync to the device.

- Video – this area will contain any video files you sync to the device, sortable by TV Show, Movie, and Home Video.

- Podcasts – this area contains a sorted listing of the podcasts you've synced to the device. We'll discuss podcasts a little later in this guide.

- Radio – this are contains the built-in FM radio, where you can choose from any local station to listen to. You can also pause live radio for up to 15 minutes, though (for obvious reasons) you can't fast-forward live radio.

- Clock – this is where the built-in clock, stopwatch, and timer reside.

- Settings – contains all of the advanced settings for the device, which we'll go over shortly.

- Audiobooks – this area will contain all of your audiobooks purchased and/or synced from iTunes. If you have no audiobooks, this item will not appear on your home screen.

- Voice Memos – this opens the application for recording and/or listening to voice memos. Your iPod Nano includes built-in recording functionality, however, you'll need to have ear pods *with* a microphone to use it, as they aren't included with the device. This item will only show up if headphones with a microphone are plugged in, or you've synced a voice memo to the device with iTunes.

- ITunes U – this is a shortcut to your iTunes U collection of educational courses. Much like podcasts, they are available (usually for free) from the iTunes Store. This item will only show up if you have iTunes U content synced to the device to display.

Now, let's take a deeper look at the settings application, where everything you might want to change about the device is located. To get started, just tap the icon labeled 'Settings', which will be located on the second home screen by default.

At the very top of the menu, you'll find an on/off button for Bluetooth. We'll get a little more in depth with Bluetooth later in this guide. Below that, you'll find general settings:

- Brightness – the brightness of your screen is fully adjustable. To maximize the battery life of your iPod Nano, set the brightness as low as possible.

- Wallpaper – you can change the background of your home screen from here. Selection is pretty limited, but designed to look good with the specific color of your device.
- Date and Time – since the iPod Nano isn't Wi-Fi capable, you may have to set the clock, date, and time zone manually. This is where you'll do that.
- Language – if you're so inclined, you can change the displayed language here. Bear in mind, however, that this will change the language for *everything.* If you're not 100% comfortable in a language other than English, it's probably best to leave this alone.
- Accessibility – for the visual and hearing impaired, the iPod Nano includes some pretty neat features – VoiceOver and Mono sound. Turning on VoiceOver will change the way you interact with the device into a voice-assisted system. For example, when tapping on a track within the music menu, a voice will read the track name. To actually play the track, you'll have to double click once the voice has finished speaking. Mono sound is for folks with hearing problems in one ear. Turning this option on will combine the sounds heard from each headphone into a single, non-separated mono mix, making sure that you don't miss any of the audio coming out of the headphones.

Below the general settings category, you'll also find setting categories for music, video, radio, and photos. These are all pretty self-explanatory, though we suggest trying the 'sound check' function in the music section. This handy little button will normalize the volume of every audio track you play, making sure that every song you listen to plays at the same level, helping you to avoid any accidental eardrum pulverizing.

As for playing your content, the controls are pretty straightforward. Once you've tapped a song, it will automatically begin playing. You'll be greeted with a screen that looks something like this:

As you can see, the screen is somewhat dominated by the cover art. At the bottom of the screen, you'll find four items you can interact with. In the middle, you'll find the play/pause button. Tap once to pause the song, tap again to begin playing.

To the left of that, you'll find the rewind/previous button. Tap this once to move to the beginning of the song. Tap it again (quickly) to move to the previous song in the list. Tap and hold it to rewind *within* the currently playing song. To the right of the play/pause button, you'll find the fast-forward/next button. Tap it once to move to the next song. Tap and hold it to fast forward within the currently playing song.

Across the bottom, you'll find the volume slider. Slide it toward the right to increase the volume, slide it to the left to decrease the volume. Tap the album artwork to open the repeat/shuffle controls.

Part Four: Getting More out of iPod Nano

Podcasts: An Overview

As we touched on briefly at the beginning of this guide, there is a wealth of free content available through iTunes that you can copy over to your iPod whenever you like. The most celebrated, and for good reason, is probably the podcast. ITunes practically invented the market for podcasts, and it shows. Let's take a quick look at how this works.

Podcasts can be anything from news programs to comedy shows, and everything in between. It's helpful to think of podcasts as the modern-day equivalent to the old time radio show, which encompassed everything from horror stories to Little Orphan Annie. Basically, anything you can serialize qualifies, and iTunes has *thousands* of them.

Podcasts, as we noted earlier, have their own iTunes mini-store. It's kind of a misnomer, as the podcasts in the store are free to download. Organizing it in store form, however, makes it really easy to browse and find the content you're looking for.

To get started with podcasts, click the iTunes Store button and then the Podcasts tab. Once you've done that, you'll be greeted with a page that looks something like this:

Feel free to browse the store in the same way you have previously for music and movies. It functions in the same way. You can also enter anything you like in the search bar or click the 'all categories' dropdown menu for a list of various podcast categories.

While most of the podcasts are audio only, some are video. You'll notice the video podcasts have a little icon next to them that looks a lot like a television. Once you've landed on something you'd like to check out, click on it to be taken to that podcast's page. For our example, we clicked on the *hugely* popular podcast "WTF with Marc Maron", a comedy/interview show that's updated twice a week.

As you can see, it's set up a lot like an album page in the music section of the iTunes store. There are tabs for details, ratings and reviews, and related items. On the left, you'll see track numbers. Hovering over these track numbers will bring up a play button. While in the music iTunes Store, this would play a 90 second preview of the track, in the podcast section it'll play the entire thing. To "purchase" individual episodes, click on the label 'free' on the right side of each track. Once you've done that, the episode will immediately begin downloading.

Alternately, you can also click the button labeled 'Subscribe' just below the podcast's picture. This will bring up the subscription dialog box:

As you can see, clicking subscribe will download the latest episode of the podcast, and then automatically download all future episodes as they are released. This is pretty convenient, saving you the trouble of searching for a podcast every time you want to download another episode.

Once you've downloaded at least one podcast, your library will now have a separate section for them:

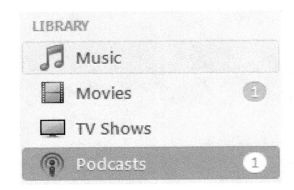

To access your podcasts, just select the 'Podcasts' item in the library menu. Once you've done that, you'll be greeted with the podcast library screen, which will look something like this:

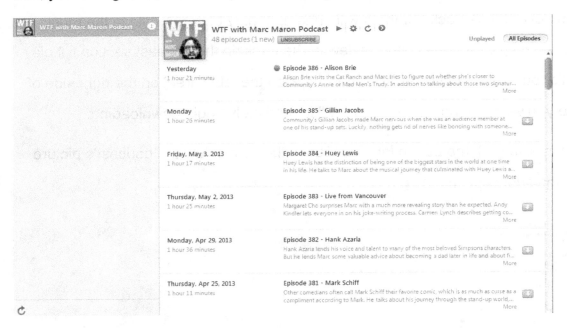

From there, you can simply drag the episode(s) you want to listen to toward the right side of the screen to copy them to your iPod. You can also sync the podcast to your device by tabbing over to the podcast view' on your iPod summary page and clicking 'Sync Podcasts'

This will copy all new, un-played episodes of your podcasts to your device whenever it's plugged in. From there, you'll find them under the 'Podcasts' menu on your iPod Nano.

All about Fitness

Since the iPod Nano is such a great device for the active, outdoorsy, running enthusiast type, Apple added some pretty neat functionality in that vein. Let's take a quick moment to investigate the fitness functions of your iPod Nano, shall we?

To get started with Fitness, tap the Fitness icon to open the program. Once you've done that, you'll be greeted with this screen:

As you can see, there are a couple of different items available here. The first thing we're going to do is enter in our data. To do this, tap the 'info' icon on the bottom right part of the screen. From there, tap the menu item labeled 'personal info' and enter in your height and weight by flicking the dials.

Once you've done that, you can interact with the fitness app in a few different ways. First, the

Nano functions as a pedometer, counting the steps you take while walking. It'll do this in the background, so you can continue to use your iPod throughout the day. In fact, after we set it up, you'll only know that it's counting steps because a little shoe icon will appear on the top of the screen next to the battery icon.

To activate this feature, find the menu item under 'Personal Info' labeled 'Walk'. From there, tap the button to turn on 'Daily Step Goal' and choose a number. Once you've done that, exit the menu by flicking to the right, and then tap the icon labeled 'Walk.' A screen that looks like this will appear:

From here, just press the Start button, and go about your day. The iPod Nano will automatically count the steps you take, the amount of time you've been walking, the distance you've done, and the (estimated) calories you've burned doing it. For the most accurate step counting, keep the Nano as near to your waist as possible.

Now, if you want to get a little more fit, you can also use the iPod Nano as a run/workout tracker. This has a couple of added features compared to the walk/pedometer functionality – you can choose your music, and select a workout type/duration.

To set this up, just tap the 'Run' icon on the fitness home screen. From there, you'll be presented with a screen that looks like this:

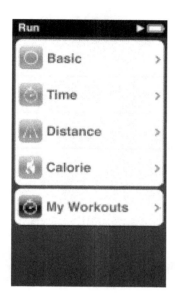

From here, you can choose workouts based on the time you've got, the distance you'd like to run, the calories you'd like to burn, or just choose basic for a random run with no end in sight. Once you've chosen those parameters, you'll be given the opportunity to choose a playlist, some music from your device, the radio, a podcast, or an iTunes U course to listen to while you're running.

Once you've chosen something, you'll be taken back to the 'Run' screen. Press start and begin the workout. The iPod Nano will inform you (by voice) when you've reached your goal. Pause the workout at any time using the controls on the side of the device.

Now, once you've completed a workout, that information is saved for you. Tap the history button on the lower left side of the fitness home screen to get a look at the workouts you've done. If you're *really* into keeping track of these workouts, you can also plug your device back into your computer and open iTunes after a workout. Once you've used the fitness program, you'll be greeted with this screen the next time you plug the device in:

To enable this functionality, click 'Send'. After a few moments, your data will be uploaded to

the Nike+ website, and you'll be greeted with another pop-up:

To keep track of your Nike+ stats, you'll need to create an account. Begin the process by

clicking 'Visit'. Once you've done that, a browser window will open, taking you to the Nike+

website, and congratulating you on your first workout:

From there, find the 'Sign Up' button on the top right of the browser window and fill out the information. Voila! You're officially a member of Nike+, ready to track your workouts along with millions of other fitness enthusiasts.

Conclusion

Well, there you have it: the iPod Nano. We're pretty sure there's never been a device that packs so much interesting stuff into such a tiny little package. We've shown you the ins and outs – setting up the software, working with videos and podcasts, and a whole lot more. We hope that you've learned a little something, but more importantly, we hope that we've helped to instill in you the confidence to treat this device like anything else – not as something to be feared, but as something to be explored, played with, and, above all else, enjoyed.

We're sure you'll be getting a lot of use out of your new iPod Nano, and we hope you've enjoyed reading this guide half as much as we've enjoyed writing it.

Thanks for reading!

About Minute Help Press

Minute Help Press is building a library of books for people with only minutes to spare. Follow @minutehelp on Twitter to receive the latest information about free and paid publications from Minute Help Press, or visit minutehelpguides.com.

www.ingramcontent.com/pod-product-compliance
Lightning Source LLC
Chambersburg PA
CBHW082112070326
40689CB00052B/4618